Rubbing Elbows

poems by

DeMisty D. Bellinger

Finishing Line Press
Georgetown, Kentucky

Rubbing Elbows

Copyright © 2017 by DeMisty D. Bellinger
ISBN 978-1-63534-284-0 First Edition
All rights reserved under International and Pan-American Copyright Conventions.
No part of this book may be reproduced in any manner whatsoever without written permission from the publisher, except in the case of brief quotations embodied in critical articles and reviews.

ACKNOWLEDGMENTS

"Yoko Ono Said" and "What Did You Mean To" appeared in *Unbroken Journal*. "I Guide Stevie Wonder by the Hand" and "Play Date: Tina Turner | Janis Joplin" appeared in *Modern Poetry Quarterly Review*. "Jimi Hendrix and I Wait Together" and "A Treatise on My Ignorance, in which I Wallow Happily, Blissfully" appeared separately in *Eunoia Review*. "King of Pop Sonnet," "Conversations with Whitney over Colas," and "The Grooming of a Pop Star" appeared in *Former People: Bangs, Whimpers, Arts, Culture, and Commentary*. "Woman Slowly Dying" and "The House That Has Eight Grandkids" first appeared in *The Tau Journal*. "Misterioso" and "The Unrequited Love Story of Mary Mallon" appeared in *Blue Fifth Review*.

Thank you, Vermont Studio Center for allowing me a full month to write.

Thank you, Neal, for being first reader and first critic, always, I love you!

Publisher: Leah Maines

Editor: Christen Kincaid

Cover Art: Charisse Renee

Author Photo: Neal Delfeld

Cover Design: Elizabeth Maines

Printed in the USA on acid-free paper.
Order online: www.finishinglinepress.com
        also available on amazon.com

Author inquiries and mail orders:
Finishing Line Press
P. O. Box 1626
Georgetown, Kentucky 40324
U. S. A.

Table of Contents

I Guide Stevie Wonder by the Hand 1

The Grooming of a Pop Star 2

Many Troubled Hours 3

What Did You Mean To 4

Polonaises and Pastorals 5

Yoko Ono Said 6

Jimi Hendrix and I Wait Together 7

The Unrequited Love Story of Mary Mallon 8

Play Date: Tina Turner | Janis Joplin 9

Misterioso 10

King of Pop Sonnet 11

Madonna's Letters 12

Conversations with Whitney over Colas 13

Bus ride: Barack Obama, Marilyn Monroe 14

El Paso 15

Rubbing Elbows 16

Woman Slowly Dying 17

The House That Has Eight Grandkids 18

A Treatise on My Ignorance, in which
    I Wallow Happily, Blissfully 19

Orlando 20

for my parents, Maxine and Laurence,
who have encouraged me to stay curious and unsatisfied.

I Guide Stevie Wonder by the Hand

I wait patiently at the corner, watching lights
I say nothing, but walk. He walks.
His hand is slim in mine, cold and dry.
He doesn't know it, but the color collects in the bed of his fingernails:
This is where he is blackest.
I guide him around a corner
The building with cinder glass obscures what's inside
I imagine rich people there
I say, "rich white people, but we can't see them working."
I nudge him a little and he steps a little higher, avoiding
Legs laying out on the sidewalk, splayed
Brown bagged bottle between them.
Beside the bakery
We smell nuts and caramel cooking
I tell him that everything is beautiful:
Cakes tiered for weddings, cookies decked out for celebrations,
candies small and brown.
"Rich white people dressed in furs and cashmere, flashing bills I can't
 recognize."
I walk him further and slow my step over ice
Around dog shit
       His nose wrinkles
We are near the park and I angle him—
We walk across the block long park.
The grass is crunchy with winter.
In the exact middle of the park,
Stevie stops me,
We stand still and my heart feels too violent.
He says, "Listen. Just shhh."

The Grooming of a Pop Star

I'm sure she knew nothing of Johnathan Swift
Or she did—
Obsessed with Gulliver's Travels and Lilliputian and soft boiled eggs
    cracked on which end
She came up with satires extended into pages
She's political as all that and,
        When she was twelve
            She spoke in an affected British accent.

I'm sure she danced like a cow with three left hooves when she was fourteen
She refused to go with Robby G. Glick for the homecoming dance because
She could not do even the simplest white girl bop
So she stayed home and watched television
Party of Five then the Gilmore Girls.

I'm sure she sang in the shower, the choir, the car, the bus, in tune, always,
    in tune
And turned heads
When she closed her eyes, she'd imagine herself wearing red lipstick
that glimmered and sparkled
and light bounced off it, off her, off her eyes, she glowed, she was
Taylor Swift

Many Troubled Hours

Clara's wearing too tight shoes.
Robert has fucked up his hands real good, but
Clara's feet hurt. And her chest was weak from the corset.
And my god, was she pregnant again?
She stood up real slow and gave Richard a look like,
"I dare you to say a word, motherfucker."
She went into the restroom and collapsed on the fainting couch,
Thinking of Johannes, she let her eyes close against the ugly
English girls singing nasally in the mirror. They were
Mocking *Lohengrin* and Clara
Almost laughed.

What Did You Mean To

I think she says to not call her lady or Lady aloud or in her head or in my head and I say aloud—maybe too loudly, "to your right, Miss Holiday," and she does. I inhale and taste the jungles of everywhere on my lips, my teeth. I tell her this. I say, aloud (or in one of our heads), "I taste what we'll fight for years ahead of now. You heard of Kennedy? You heard of war?" She looks at me and laughs, and in it, I hear her every sorrow, every yearning, and I understand then why "April in Paris" makes me both giddily-girl happy and practicing what my therapist will define years later as suicide ideation, but what I'd hear is suicidation. "Miss Holiday," I say

Polonaises and Pastorals

Amantine-Lucile-Aurore,
wrapped in ink-stained throws
leans towards the fireplace to
watch Frédéric play the piano.

Wind whirls into the castle's cracks.
Not quite a castle, but a monastery.
A place made for silences:
walls thick, floors cold,
rooms robbed of mirth and merriment,

Still in it she writes.
He composes.
They create silent noises.

The blowing air is constant—
music from his stands and
writings from her desk
flutter in the breezes and fall to the floor.
Aurore would pick up a sheet of his,
mixed with a sheet of hers.

She refuses to understand the little
perfect circles at the end of stems.
She chooses instead to see the notes as plants
growing from black stems,
staves as grasses shadowed across the fields and
clefs as flowers we cannot eat.

Yoko Ono Said

Yoko Ono said that I could not have really loved The Beatles and that I didn't know John Lennon. "Did you cry when he died?" I explained to Ms. Ono that I was not alive when Lennon was shot. She said, "Oh." The word made her lips, painted spilling-blood red, round out into an oval. Bumps there. A faint mustache, or the absence of a mustache. Pores. "Do you know love?" she said. I asked Ms. Ono if she was, seriously, asking me such a useless question. She stepped back and laughed. I said to her that I believed in her like little kids believed in beastly beings beneath their beds. She, then, stepped forward. Towards me. I told her that The Beatles was already dead when she arrived. She smiled. Lipstick on her teeth.

Jimi Hendrix and I Wait Together

I won't use any of the clichés to describe his hands, his fingers—
such as sculpted or tapered or birdlike—but I will say that
they looked capable of tearing hard fruit in half,
of splitting bread for a crowd,
I will say that his fingers were defined as if manufactured and certain,
the nails short and clean,
muscles appeared on the left hand where I assumed no muscles could
    form,
I can say that the color on his hands was uniform and calming as if it,
    too,
the color of creamy Creole coffee,
was pertinent to his playing.

You can find pictures and pictures of his smile flashing his teeth and
    see them,
bold and square and shining back at the camera.
You can close your eyes and hear his goofy laugh.
I don't have to describe his smile.

"It worked itself out in my head when I was on the toilet."
The rhythm of this sentence started slow and sped up.
Everything about him, musical, musical, musical.
Who meets at bus stops in Wisconsin?
He said, "I dig The Beatles, too. People don't know what me and Paul
    have."
Who meets in bus stops in Wisconsin?
We do. That is how we met.

The Unrequited Love Story of Mary Mallon

Everyone cries but Mary, who moves with lifted head above the famished crowd. Everyone is too miserable to know they're hungry. It is Mary who can't stop eating, won't stop cooking. She grows bigger, hips knocking boney patrons who come to dine, but can't bring themselves to order or worse, leave food congealing on their plates. Mary busses the tables she served and hidden in the kitchen, eats their wasted food without fork, unknowingly recreating the taste of salt on his skin.

Play Date: Tina Turner | Janis Joplin

I painted her toenails blue
Though the bottle said "azure"
We say this word "azure" aloud
Exaggerating the 'Z'
And share sounds that make our lips
Pucker.
I blow air on her toes
She blows air across the waves.

Misterioso

Monk's goatee pointed somewhere over my shoulder
   I turned and looked where it was directing me and saw
      floating in the café
         half-tones and tritones and seconds bleeding through the air.
I didn't think they'd look like that.
   I had imagined music to look as it is notated
      (fat balls with erect tails)
         but music is fuller and amorphous and polychromatic.
The word synæsthesia came to mind.
   I couldn't hear the music Monk played anymore,
      just the after-tones:
         notes not found in a single piano key,
         but resounding in the case and against the harp.
   I couldn't concentrate anymore.
I followed the sound to an altar covered in purple and lavender and black.
Knelt on a prayer bench covered in red velvet and, to hear
clearer, took a vow of silence.

King of Pop Sonnet

Michael Jackson no longer feels highs and
Lows and barbs at his demeanor, his looks.
No longer sings in falsettos or cries out
In jubilant syllables, "hee," or "hoo."
Michael Jackson's worries of tabloid covers,
Billboards, ratings: gone. His skin—sepia
or stained deck browns—concerns no one.
And he hides his love life from no one here.

Michael Jackson is weary of the sea now,
but at peace and the sun is warm and the
living so easy. If he wanted to
he could spit up into the air, arcing
the spittle across the bow of the boat
watch it glitter like so many studded gloves.

Madonna's Letters

Madonna didn't write me when I asked her to, when I channeled her from the Midwest hoping the waters in those Great Lakes would wave my words to her, Midwest Michigan—here's Detroit, and do you remember Detroit? This is where rough white kids who make it big come from. She didn't send a letter, but she looked at me over television fuzz of "Kid Video," lace and mascara and lipstick and mole and boldness that only rough white kids from the Midwest hold, and I told my sister, "She's looking at me." My sister, who believed anything, believed me, too.

Conversations with Whitney over Colas

Talk about the gaucheness of hotel bathtubs.
Do not mention hotel bathtubs.
Say nothing of hotels.
Expound on the importance of family and children, but
refrain from using the word "future."
Make eye contact and make her laugh.
Do not smoke in front of her.
Do not smack your teeth in front of her.
Do not mention men who go freely before
cameras and boasts around her. Do not
talk of men. Do not talk of awards or the coolness
of bathtubs, the porcelain ungiven, the water
hot as blood, the bubbles
dissipating before the bath is
over.

Bus ride: **Barack Obama**
                         Marilyn Monroe

He asks about the other president
    With the Boston Accent
        Speaking German when German speaking was
unfashionable
She laughs, feigning forgetfulness.
Harmless flirtation on his part, on her part.
That is what these people do: Flirt.

She hums a tune he can't quite place.
    He asks her about it
    She can't remember
"It's been so long!"
Without pain or worry—
Laughing like Southern Sundays spread out over summer.

El Paso

American fuckers keep thinking they'll find Felina,
Looking at our eyes for blackness,
Touching our hair as if it belonged to them.

"You packing heat, cowboy?"
We drink their pockets dry.
They pass us dollar bills and we stuff them in our bustiers.
They look down our dresses,
Hoping they can follow each cent.

We smile.
Our eyes are not black,
Our eyes are not evil.

We rub against them,
Rub them.
Watch them not handle their tequila.
Watch them wither on barstools.
Watch their eyelids flutter:
They dream they are at Rose's.

Rubbing Elbows

In the city, stars timidly show in the twilight sky and
I point out the planets to you.
"Let's walk," I say, "until the city lights
Dim behind us inconsequentially. Let's
Cast ourselves among these unattainable places. Here,
We don't have to pretend notoriety;
It can be enough to rub elbows with the stars.
I can wear my best dress and here,
I'll lend you something."
But we walk only a mile or so then,
Turn back. Still—
My elbows are dry and bruised
From the quick tour.

Woman Slowly Dying

Her head is too big for her shoulders
and her hair is too big for her head.

She walks as if her toes all depend
on the second toe and her toenails are too long.

Too big for this century, with her
curls creeping over her back

Over her face, her shoulders, reaching
down into her bosom, tresses like fingers.

Her hair shines like only sable could:
iridescent and too bright in the sun.

This is how a crow is beautiful—
kaleidoscopic colors, all concentrated in black.

This is how she is beautiful—
decaying bit by bit like a magic show.

The House That Has Eight Grandkids

Has, too, a reticent man
Who keeps his lawn
Immaculate
With flowering trees for
Song birds;

Has too, two little dogs
Barking in syncopation
With my footfalls and the traffic
From Summer Street;

And has
a grandmotherly woman
Who gives us cookies in December,
questioning our religion.

A Treatise on My Ignorance, in which I Wallow Happily, Blissfully

I know enough to admire the beauty of:
      uneven spaces on a page; punctuation creating patterns, creating ways, creating paths; repeated words, implied sighs, colors contrasting on screen, on printed page, between the white of the eye and the rest of it; someone else's music in someone else's car, growing louder as they come nearer, growing fainter as they drive away, the singer's words never clear—lyrics I'll never know to a song I'll never hear again; the upstairs neighbors running around, upstairs, jumping around, yelling, composing together a noise that is singular; a joyful noise not music made by people I do not like at all.

Orlando

> *"Sometimes I feel like throwing my hands up in the air"*
> —Florence + the Machine

> *"Oh, make me wanna holler/ And throw up both my hands"*
> —Marvine Gaye

I want the biggest party
I want every dj ever to make a playlist
I want sparkly makeup and glow sticks,
Whistles and noisemakers
I want to have to yell over the music
I want to stop dancing but I don't want to stop dancing
I want to feel the floor bounce beneath me
I want driving basslines paving the way
I want everything colored rainbow, rainbow, rainbow
I want salsa music and merengue and samba
I want it to be so humid and sweaty and hot that my hair sticks to my face,
To your face, others' faces covered in glitter
I want to see teeth glowing in the black light
I want to be sprayed with water
I want tropical drinks
I want breaks in the music where I can catch secrets screamed over non-noise
Then I want the music to come in louder than before
I want to holler woo, throw up both my hands
I want happiness to be tactile, kinetic, joining us like scales on fish
I want men kissing men and men kissing men and men kissing men
I want women kissing women and women kissing women
I want to kiss everyone
I want the biggest party and to see everybody dance now
In June, in Florida,
Where the sunrises are the color of Elizabeth Bishop's dreams
I want the sun to always rise
I want to know there will be a tomorrow

Notes

"Many Troubled Hours" comes from a line from the shared diaries between Clara and Robert Schumann, in which she writes in regards to her husband's depression in 1841, "I was very irritable and because of this gave myself many troubled hours."

George Sand and Frederick Chopin co-habited in an old monastery for some time.

Mary Mallon is better known as Typhoid Mary, who was a carrier of the typhoid disease but did not suffer from it.

In the song "April in Paris," Billie Holiday sings, "What did you mean to / What have you done to / my heart?"

"Misterioso" is a song by Thelonious Monk, in which he plays with tritones and dissonance.

Singer Whitney Houston was found dead in her hotel room's bathtub.

"El Paso" is in response to Marty Robbins' lyrics to the song by the same name.

On June 12, 2016, forty-nine people were killed and fifty-three people were injured at the Pulse dance hall in Orlando, Florida.

DeMisty D. Bellinger was born and raised in Milwaukee. She went to the magnet schools that focused on art and graduated from the Milwaukee High School of the Arts. After taking a year off, DeMisty studied English at the University of Wisconsin-Platteville. She went on to receive an MFA in Creative Writing from Southampton College on Long Island, NY, and a Ph.D. from the University of Nebraska-Lincoln, where she focused on creative writing in fiction. In 2012, she attended Bread Loaf Writers Conference for fiction.

DeMisty earned many accolades for her writing, including the Mari Sandoz/Prairie Schooner Award in Short Fiction while she was a student in Nebraska and a Vermont Studio Center fellowship in 2015. Her short-short, "Tiger Free Days," was listed in the Wigleaf Top 50 Very Short Fictions of 2014.

Many of her poems, short stories, and essays can be found online in various publications, including *Helen, Necessary Fiction, Driftless Review, WhiskeyPaper, Blue Fifth Review,* and *Former People: A Journal of Bangs and Whimpers*. You can find links to many of her works at demistybellinger.com.

Besides writing fiction, DeMisty plays viola with a community orchestra, raises twin girls with her loving husband, and teaches Creative Writing at Fitchburg State University in Massachusetts.